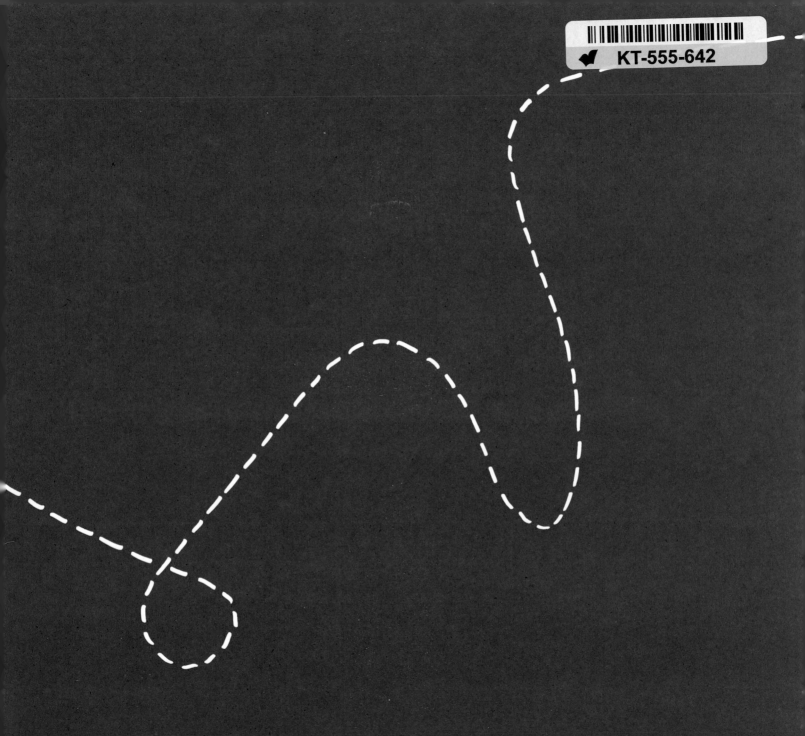

BUSY PLACES

School

Carol Watson

Fife
C O U N C I L
King's Road **Primary School**

W
FRANKLIN WATTS
NEW YORK • LONDON • SYDNEY

It is 6.30 in the morning.
Mr O'Sullivan,
the School Caretaker,
opens up the school gates.

Next he sweeps the
playground before
the parents and
children arrive.

Inside the school building,
Mr Joseph is busy cleaning the classrooms.
He polishes the tables and
makes the rooms neat and tidy.

At 7.30 a.m. the teachers start to arrive.
They have a lot of work to do before the children come to school.

4

Some of the teachers
cover tables,
put out pots of glue
and prepare for
an art activity.
Mrs Tuohy collects
information books
from the library.

At 8.45 a.m. parents
and children gather
in the playground.
The bell rings.
"Time to go into school,"
say the children.

While everyone goes into class, Miss Ransley, the Headteacher, talks to a school governor.

"I like your ideas for our Open Day," he says.

In the Nursery the children are
singing and making music.
"Hold the triangle string in one hand,
Ahmed," says Miss Cobbold, "and
play it with the other."

The children in Pink Class start the day by
weighing, measuring and using maths apparatus.
A parent helps a group of children
with their work.

Meanwhile, in Red Class some children are writing and others are reading their storybooks.

"Good, Jack," says Mrs Walker, "you read that very well."

The children in
Green Class are
painting pictures.

Mrs Stevens,
their teacher,
helps a child
to draw on
the computer.

During the morning there is assembly in the hall. Everyone claps as some of the children receive awards for working hard and good behaviour.

In the office the School Administrator answers the telephone and takes messages for the Headteacher.

The Bursar works on her computer. She looks after the money spent by the school.

During the break,
the staff have coffee and
chat. Mrs Woodcock,
the Welfare Assistant,
bathes a child who is hurt.
"There you are Alex,"
she says. "You'll feel
better now."

Later a van
brings the hot lunches
to the school.
The kitchen staff
unload the tins of food
and prepare for lunch
in the school hall.

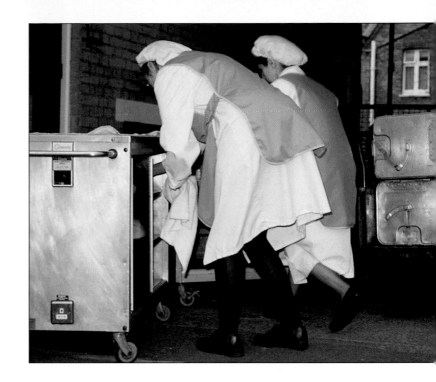

Now it's time to eat.
Some children have
hot meals,
while others bring
their own food
in their lunch boxes.

The Midday Supervisors
watch over the children at play time.
"Your turn now to have a skip,"
says Miss Gilbert.

While the children play,
Mrs Davis holds a meeting with the
Year 2 teachers. They talk about
giving extra help to some of the children
in their classes.

In the afternoon,
Turquoise Class
visit the library
to change
their books.

"I think you'd like
this story," Mrs King
tells Samantha.

Lime Class are doing
gym in the hall.
They jump on and off
the apparatus and
climb up the ropes.

At the end of the day
Miss Clark tells Blue Class a story.
The children listen carefully and
look at the pictures.
"And do you know what happened next?"
the teacher asks.

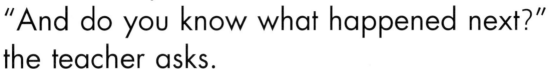

It's home time!
The teachers help
the children fasten
their coats.
It's the end
of a very
busy day.

Care and safety in school

When you are in a busy school it is important to make sure that you and others keep safe.

Try to remember some of these tips:

1. Be kind and caring to each other.
2. Follow the school codes.
3. Look after your own belongings and everything in the school.
4. Stay with your teacher until you are collected.
5. If you see a stranger wandering about the school, tell your teacher.

Index

King's Road Primary School
Rosyth - Tel: 313470

© 1997 Watts Books
96 Leonard Street
London
EC2A 4RH

Franklin Watts Australia
14 Mars Road
Lane Cove
NSW 2066

ISBN 0 7496 2792 1

Dewey Decimal Classification Number
371

A CIP catalogue record for this book is
available from the British Library

Printed in Hong Kong

Editor: Samantha Armstrong
Designer: Kirstie Billingham
Photographer: Harry Cory-Wright
Illustrations: Kim Woolley

With thanks to all the members of Strand-
on-the-Green Infant and Nursery School,
Chiswick, London.

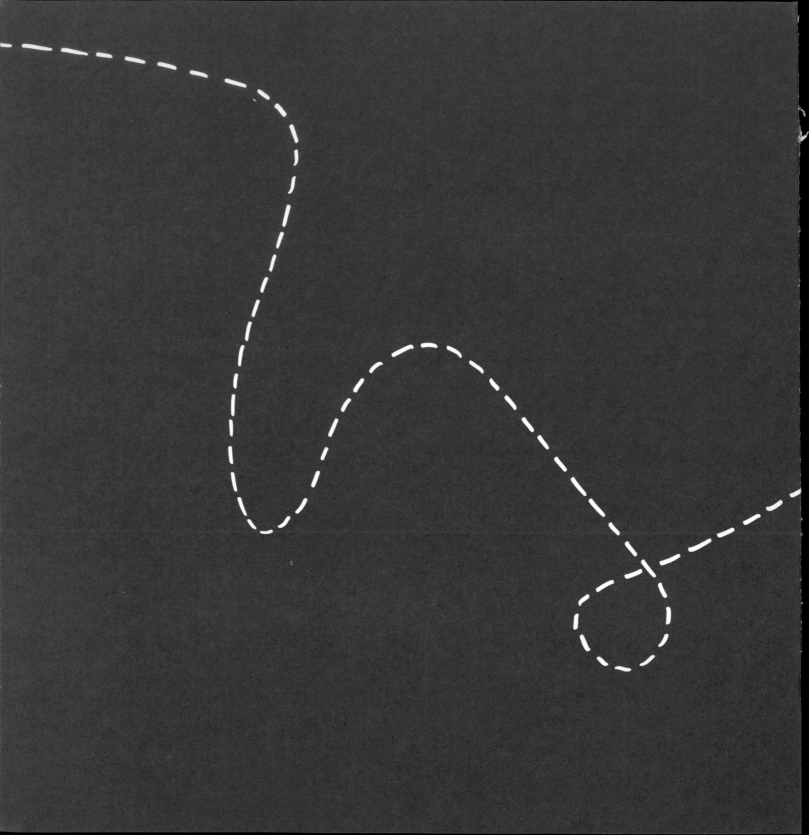